Entertainment

Paul Dowswell

www.heinemann.co.uk/library

Visit our website to find out more information about Heinemann Library books.

To order:

 Phone 44 (0) 1865 888066

Send a fax to 44 (0) 1865 314091

 Visit the Heinemann Bookshop at www.heinemann.co.uk/library to browse our catalogue and order online.

First published in Great Britain by Heinemann Library, Halley Court, Jordan Hill, Oxford OX2 8EJ, a division of Reed Educational and Professional Publishing Ltd. Heinemann is a registered trademark of Reed Educational & Professional Publishing Limited.

OXFORD MELBOURNE AUCKLAND JOHANNESBURG BLANTYRE
GABORONE IBADAN PORTSMOUTH NH (USA) CHICAGO

© Reed Educational and Professional Publishing Ltd 2001
The moral right of the proprietor has been asserted.

Designed by Tinstar Design (www.tinstar.co.uk)
Illustrations by Nicholas Beresford-Davies and Martin Griffin
Originated by Ambassador Litho Ltd
Printed in Hong Kong/China

ISBN 0431 13233 X
05 04 03 02 01
10 9 8 7 6 5 4 3 2 1

British Library Cataloguing in Publication Data
Dowswell, Paul
    Entertainment. – (Great Inventions)
    1. Recreation – History 2. Leisure – History
    I. Title
    790

Acknowledgements
The Publishers would like to thank the following for permission to reproduce photographs:
Action Comics: p15; AKG: p7; Bridgeman Art Library: pp6, 8, 9, 10, Royal Asiatic Society p6; Corbis: pp4, 11, 20, 28, 35; Gareth Boden: p5; Hulton Getty: p23, 39; Kobal Collection: p26; Mary Evans Picture Library: pp12, 14; Photodisc: p40; Redferns: p32, p33; Science and Society: pp17, 18, 19, 21, 24, 27, 30, 31, 34, 37; Yiorgos Nikiteas: p42

Cover photographs: Corbis (l), Dixons (tr), Photodisc (br)

Any words appearing in the text in bold, **like this**, are explained in the Glossary.

Contents

Introduction

Fifteen of the nineteen items in this book were invented over the last 150 years. This is partly to do with the arrival of electricity, which had a massive effect on every area of people's lives. Only the camera and record player did not use electricity when they first appeared, but cameras now have electrically-powered microcircuits and record players went electric in the 1920s.

Leisure time

This boom in entertainment inventions was also prompted by the amount of leisure time people had. Before the 20th century, most people in developed countries worked 60–70 hours a week. The idea of the 'weekend' only arrived in the 19th century. Previous to this, Sunday, as set out in the Bible, had been the only day of rest. But even then, people were expected to spend much of their free time going to church.

A Victorian Music Hall performance. Music Hall was the last form of mass entertainment before electricity arrived.

Until the last century families were much larger than they are now, and women who didn't work found their time almost completely taken up with childcare and housework. (Lack of effective birth control meant larger families, as did terrible rates of death in childhood. Couples tended to have more children to ensure at least some of them would survive to adulthood.)

Up until the end of the 19th century, entertainment was generally a sociable activity. People played cards or board games with friends, drank in public houses, danced at fairs and festivals and visited the theatre.

In Elizabethan England, going to see a play was something all levels of society did for entertainment. Reading though, was very much a middle class pursuit, until the education reforms and changing attitudes of Victorian times meant entire populations could read and write for the first time in history. A major publishing industry producing comics, magazines, newspapers and books sprang up to cater for this huge army of new readers.

Electricity – a revolution

Electricity began to make its presence felt in people's homes in the late 19th and early 20th centuries. Along with electric lights, electric cookers and electric fires came radios, and as the century wore on, record players, televisions, video games and others.

Entertainment outside the home was also revolutionized by electricity. Music Hall (theatrical entertainment which featured singers, comedians, magicians and all sorts of 'variety acts') was replaced by the arrival of the cinema. Dance halls were filled with louder, rowdier music, made possible by the invention of the microphone and **public address system**, and the electrification of instruments such as the guitar, double bass and organ.

Technology has created a huge choice of entertainment activities.

These days, the entertainment industry generates billions of dollars, and most of the world's most admired people are entertainers. In the Western world at least, there has never been so much leisure time, and so many leisure pursuits on offer.

Chess, c. 600

Chess is one of the oldest and most popular games in the world, though there are many different claims as to which country it came from. An Indian game called *Chaturanga* can be traced back to 2500BC. It had pieces similar to the chess pieces of the king, knight, bishop, rook and pawn, but there were four players and a dice was thrown to determine how the game should proceed. A similar game was also played in China.

A well-travelled game

The game spread along the Silk Road – a trade route between China and the Eastern Mediterranean. Different rules were developed wherever it went, although the game kept its basic character. In Burma, major pieces could go anywhere behind the front line of pawns. In Japan captured pieces could change sides. In China the king was called a general because the Chinese emperor had executed two players when he found out that his rank was being represented by a lowly **ivory** figure.

The game became popular in Persia (now called Iran), where it was known as *Chatrang*, then spread throughout the Arab world. By this time, the rules and pieces were more like the game we know today.

This engraving shows two Persian chess players. The game was very popular in Persia, and spread via the Arab world to Europe in the early Middle Ages.

The Arabs called it *Shatranj* and they took it with them into Europe, when a Muslim people called the Moors invaded Spain in 711. Chess also arrived in Europe via the Vikings. One of the most famous chess sets of the ancient world is the 'Lewis' chess men, left in Scotland's Orkney Islands by Viking settlers.

During the Middle Ages the queen and bishops were weak pieces, and it was only in the 16th century that the queen became the most powerful figure on the board. During the 18th and 19th centuries, chess became the game we play today.

Computer chess

Chess-playing computer 'Deep Thought', named after the super-computer in Douglas Adams' famous book *The Hitch-Hikers Guide to the Galaxy*, beat a world-class 'Grand Master' in 1988. World champion Gary Kasparov won a game with the same computer in 1996 (it was now known as 'Deep Blue'), but then lost a rematch in 1997. Computers can calculate up to 700,000 moves a second, whereas the best human players only think three or four moves ahead.

Pieces from the Viking 'Lewis' Chess set. Craftsmen have long played with the traditional chess shapes, and today's novelty chess sets are nothing new.

2500BC	6TH CENTURY AD	711	1958	1997
CHATURANGA, THE DISTANT ANCESTOR OF CHESS, FIRST PLAYED IN INDIA	PERSIAN GAME OF CHATRANG, SIMILAR TO CHESS PLAYED TODAY, TAKEN UP BY INVADING MUSLIMS	MUSLIMS INVADE SPAIN, AND BRING CHESS TO EUROPE	COMPUTER DEVELOPED THAT CAN PLAY CHESS	'DEEP BLUE' COMPUTER BEATS WORLD CHESS CHAMPION GARY KASPAROV

Playing cards, c. 969

Aside from watching television or listening to the radio, no other leisure activity is more popular than playing cards. This is partly to do with their versatility. There are 52 different cards in every pack, with four 'suits', each numbered one to ten, plus a jack, queen and king. Cards have been used to devise hundreds of different games, from blackjack to solitaire.

Dodgy dealings

One of the first mentions of cards in European history came in 1377, in a sermon condemning gambling. Our understanding of when playing cards reached Europe is based on laws passed to prohibit or restrict the use of cards in gambling.

Cards are also used to tell fortunes, with the Ace of Spades signifying death. Tarot cards, more commonly used in fortune telling today, were originally used in an Italian card game invented around 1440.

Origins

The origin of playing cards is shrouded in mystery. Some stories say the Crusaders brought them back from the Middle East in the early 1300s. Others say that gypsies brought them to Europe when they arrived there around 1400. Yet more stories say that famous Italian explorer Marco Polo brought them back from China in the late 13th century. Historians now think all these theories are wrong, and that playing cards first arrived in Europe around 1370, probably from Egypt.

But playing cards originally came from much further east. They were almost certainly invented in China, and the earliest recorded reference to them is in 969. Cards predating European versions have also been found in India and Japan.

Many countries had different suits for their playing cards. These are Venetian playing cards from 1758.

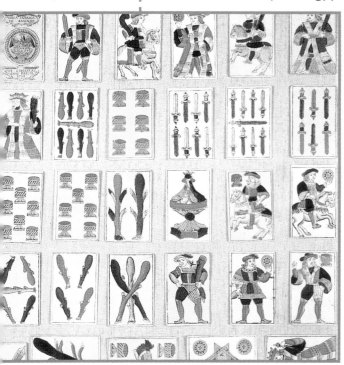

The first European playing cards were all hand-made and painted, and were so expensive only the very rich could afford them. But by 1400 **block-printing** techniques had made them readily affordable, though it took hundreds of years for the deck to settle into the 52-card format.

National suits

Suits differed from country to country. The Italians and Spanish, for example, had swords, batons, cups and coins for their symbols, and the Swiss had shields, flowers, bells and acorns. French, and later English cards had hearts, clubs, spades and diamonds, and this format was the one that eventually spread throughout the world. In the 19th century, American manufacturers introduced the familiar satin-finish and rounded corners we know today, and the joker was invented in 1850 for a game called Euchre.

This 16th century painting shows four men playing cards. They are using the French style cards, which used hearts, clubs, diamonds and spades as suits.

969	1370s	1440	1480s	1850
FIRST MENTION OF PLAYING CARDS, IN CHINA	PLAYING CARDS ARRIVE IN SPAIN AND ITALY, FROM EGYPT	TAROT CARD GAME INVENTED IN ITALY	SPADES, HEARTS, CLUBS AND DIAMONDS SUITS APPEAR ON FRENCH PLAYING CARDS	JOKER INVENTED

Fireworks, c. 1000

Fireworks are a combination of chemicals designed to produce light and noise. They were made possible by the discovery of gunpowder – a mixture of the chemicals potassium nitrate, charcoal and sulphur. Most historians agree that fireworks were invented by the Chinese around 1000 years ago. Made from hollow bamboo stalks and rolled paper tubes stuffed with gunpowder, they would be used to scare off evil spirits, and to celebrate births, weddings, anniversaries and the New Year.

Quite independently from the Chinese, English monk and scientist Roger Bacon discovered gunpowder in 1242. He mixed together a precise combination of the same three chemicals used in China, and noted '...if you light it, you will get thunder and lightening if you know the trick.'

The Chinese used gunpowder against the invading Mongols in 1279, to propel war rockets. Europeans made firearms and cannons with it. Firemakers, employed by an army to manufacture gunpowder, were also called upon to make fireworks to celebrate victories.

Growing popularity

Italian firemakers were said to be the best in Europe and they were making fireworks in Florence in the 1400s. Elaborate plaster figures were made with orange sparks cascading from their mouth and eyes. By the 16th century, fireworks were popular in England. Henry VIII's second wife Anne Boleyn had a wedding procession in 1533, which featured a group of men carrying flaming fireworks on poles.

A painting of fireworks over the River Arno, Italy in the 19th century.

Fireworks crossed the Atlantic with the first North American settlers. In the United States, the first Independence Day celebrations in 1777 were marked with firework displays.

Fireworks of many colours

In the 1830s, Italian firework makers discovered that a chemical called potassium chlorate added to the standard gunpowder mix would make a firework burn faster and hotter. This meant that they could add chemicals that did not normally burn at temperatures created by exploding gunpowder. Metal extracts could now be added to make brilliant colours and louder explosions. For example, a gold and white shower of sparks comes from iron and aluminium pellets.

Firework displays are still popular. In the United States, Independence Day is still celebrated with massive firework shows. In Britain most families celebrate Bonfire Night, to commemorate the occasion in 1605 when Guy Fawkes failed to blow up the Houses of Parliament. Some national events use tens of thousands of fireworks connected to hundreds of miles of wiring, which use electrical signals to ignite fireworks with extraordinary precision – sometimes in time to a piece of music.

Firework displays today often use computers and electrical wiring to ignite immensely complex sequences of explosions. This display in Sydney, Australia, celebrates the new millennium.

c. 1000	1242	c. 1400	1777	1830s
CHINESE DISCOVER GUNPOWDER AND MAKE FIREWORKS	GUNPOWDER DISCOVERED IN EUROPE	FIREWORKS USED IN PUBLIC CELEBRATIONS IN EUROPE	FIREWORKS USED TO CELEBRATE INDEPENDENCE DAY IN USA	USE OF NEW CHEMICAL MAKE FIREWORKS MORE COLOURFUL

Piano, 1709

People have always felt compelled to make music. Stone Age humans played music on bone flutes and mammoth skull drums. The first harps date back 6500 years to the city of Ur in Sumer. As civilizations evolved, so did musical instruments: horns and **reed instruments** were invented, and animal **intestines** were wound tight to make 'gut' strings for the **viol** and **lute**.

From harpsichord to piano

Harpsichords were first invented in the 14th century. They had a keyboard of around 50 notes, which, via a complex mechanism, plucked a tuned string. But the keyboard only played at one volume. It was not possible for a harpsichord player to play softer or louder.

In 1709 Italian harpsichord-maker Bartolomeo Cristofori invented the first piano, which was more responsive to a player's touch. He called it a *gravicembalo col pian e forte*, which means 'harpsichord with soft and loud', in Italian. Later, a French instrument maker named Sébastien Érard, invented the soft and loud pedals, which allowed a player to vary the volume of the piano even more. American Alpheus Babcock devised the first piano with an iron frame, making the instrument less fragile than the previous all-wood construction.

In the 19th century, pianos became a familiar feature in middle class living rooms.

A popular instrument

With the arrival of the piano, the harpsichord went out of fashion. Great composers, such as Mozart, leaped at the chance to write music for this new, and highly expressive instrument. The first pianos were large instruments (now known as grand pianos) and smaller ones, such as the upright piano, were made for the living rooms of the European and North American middle classes.

Piano manufacturers had a ready market for customers. In the days before radio and television, musical evenings were a very popular way of passing the time with family and friends. The piano is still a popular instrument, at home and on the concert platform, but electronic keyboards are serious rivals. They are smaller, lighter, easier to play, and a great deal more versatile, but they cannot reproduce the warm tone and responsive touch of a real piano.

Player pianos

Mechanical self-playing pianos, called 'player pianos', were invented in the early 19th century. They worked via a **pneumatic** mechanism operated by spring-driven clockwork, or by the turn of a handle. They were particularly popular in the United States. By 1920, 70% of all pianos manufactured were player pianos. The arrival of radio and gramophone records caused a rapid decline in their popularity.

How a piano key hits the string

When the key is struck, the hammer mechanism throws the hammer against the string. When the key is released, the damper mechanism stops the string from sounding.

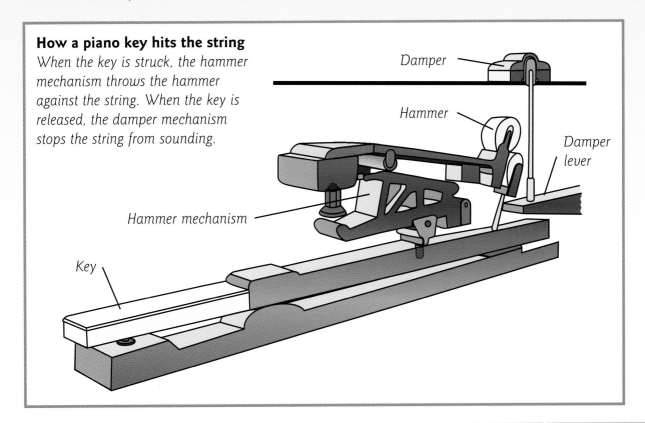

Damper

Hammer

Damper lever

Hammer mechanism

Key

1709	1770	1820	1821	1825	1876
BARTOLOMEO CRISTOFORI INVENTS PIANO	CHRISTIAN ERNST FRIEDERIC OF GERA, SAXONY, BUILDS FIRST UPRIGHT PIANO	PLAYER PIANOS INVENTED	ÉRARD INVENTED THE SOFT AND LOUD PEDALS	ALPHEUS BABCOCK DEVISES IRON FRAME PIANO	FIRST ELECTRONIC KEYBOARD 'THE MUSICAL TELEGRAPH' INVENTED BY ELISHA GRAY

Comics, c. 1850

Comics are stories told in a series of drawings – often accompanied by text boxes and speech bubbles. They've been around in one form or another at least as long as the Bayeux Tapestry of the 11th century, and some people consider early cave paintings and Egyptian hieroglyphs to be the earliest form of comic. They are called 'funnies' in the United States, suggesting that comics are created to amuse, though many also depict adventure and fantasy stories.

Politics and slap-stick

The comic-book style of **caricature** drawings and speech bubbles originated in England in the 18th century. Political cartoonists such as William Hogarth, James Gillray and Thomas Rowlandson produced drawings that mocked political issues and personalities. These were then sold in shops as single prints.

Eighteenth-century cartoonists such as James Gillray pioneered the comic style we know today, with their grotesque caricatures, and use of speech bubbles.

the PATRIOT turned PLAGARIST or the Petty Taxe Gatherers, Hunting John Bull

This style of **satire** was also popular in Europe where the comic style we know today evolved. By the mid-19th century, French and German publishers were printing **tabloid**-sized 'picture sheets'. Produced on newspaper-quality paper, and initially in black and white, they contained short, **slap-stick** stories told in a series of pictures with captions underneath.

These picture sheets were exported to the USA, to be sold to French and German immigrants there. The USA also produced its own home-grown comic at this time. The publishers D C Johnson of Boston created a comic called *Scraps* in 1849, which was very much in the same format.

Newspapers and magazines

Comics were perfect for the newly **literate** societies of Europe and North America, and soon became universally popular. Improvements in printing technology enabled newspapers and magazines to be produced in millions, and sold at a small price.

The first comic books appeared in the early 1890s, as colour **supplements** in newspapers. The subject matter was always comical, involving characters getting up to mischief. By the beginning of the 20th century, comic colour supplements were appearing in newspapers on both sides of the Atlantic, and the comic format was spreading all over the world.

It was only in the 1930s that comics containing original material began to be sold independently of newspapers. In 1938 the character Superman appeared in *Action Comics*, and made comics even more popular. This was followed by hundreds of imitations, such as Batman, Spiderman and the X-Men.

Initially produced to sell newspapers and amuse children, comics now have much broader appeal. Whether on their own or as newspaper strips, comics continue to be widely popular.

The first 'superhero', Superman took comics into another dimension as far as sales were concerned. Originally created in 1938, Superman continues to be a massive success in comic, TV and motion picture format.

18TH CENTURY	c. 1850	1890s	1938
BRITISH POLITICAL CARTOONISTS PIONEER USE OF SPEECH BUBBLES	PICTURE SHEETS BECOME POPULAR IN FRANCE AND GERMANY	AMERICAN NEWSPAPERS BEGIN TO PRODUCE COMIC COLOUR SUPPLEMENTS	SUPERMAN APPEARS IN *ACTION COMICS*, AND IS A HUGE SUCCESS

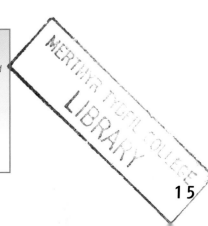

Record player, 1877

The phonograph

The first words ever recorded in human history were of American inventor Thomas Alva Edison in 1877. He shouted 'Hello, Hello,' into a recording device which he called the phonograph. Then he recited 'Mary had a little lamb.' Edison originally intended the phonograph to be a dictation machine, but it soon became a popular way of listening to speech and music.

The phonograph was the first practical sound recording and playing machine. If someone spoke or sang into the large horn, it caused a **diaphragm** at the bottom of the horn to move. This in turn made a needle vibrate, and etch a record of these vibrations onto a sheet of tin foil attached to a rotating drum. For playback, the needle retraced the indentations it had made, and this caused the diaphragm to vibrate. The horn amplified these vibrations into a sound that was loud enough to be heard.

Thomas Alva Edison (1847–1931)

Edison was one of the greatest inventors in history. Born in Ohio, USA, he had a rocky start to life – he was expelled from school aged seven, by a headmaster who thought he was 'retarded'. Edison in fact suffered from partial deafness, caused by scarlet fever.

He began his working life as a telegraph operator, but his curiosity led him into a career as an inventor. During his life he held over a thousand **patents** on his inventions, including the light bulb, the phonograph and the kinetoscope, the first moving picture machine. Edison also created and set up the electricity supply system of a central generator sending out electricity to customers via copper wires, transformers and electricity meters. He also set up the world's first industrial research laboratory, which he called his 'inventions factory', in Menlo Park, New Jersey.

The gramophone

Ten years later another American, German-born Emile Berliner, replaced the rotating drum with a flat disc and invented the gramophone – more commonly known as the record player. It soon became a popular way of listening to music at home. In 1892 Berliner also invented a method of copying discs. Previous to this, musicians and singers making records had made hundreds of recordings of a song – now they only had to make one! Between them Edison and Berliner invented the most popular form of home entertainment since the piano, and laid the foundations of the multi-billion dollar music business we know today.

In the 1920s electrical gramophones began to replace mechanical ones. These converted the vibrations of the needle into an electrical signal, which was then **amplified** by a loudspeaker, rather than a horn. A volume control allowed listeners to play their music louder or quieter, and the sound quality was a great improvement on the mechanical gramophone.

Little changed until 1948, when the Columbia record company introduced the LP (long player) record. Previous to this, gramophone discs had only four or five minutes playing time on them. LPs could hold up to 25 minutes of music per side. Cassette tapes also became popular in the 1960s and 1970s. Nowadays CDs, introduced in the early 1980s, are the most popular form of recorded music.

This phonograph was designed by Thomas Edison. It could be used for both recording and playing back speech or music. Edison famously said: 'Genius is one per cent inspiration, ninety-nine per cent perspiration.'

1877	1887	1920s	1948	1949	1980s
THOMAS EDISON INVENTS PHONOGRAPH	EMILE BERLINER INVENTS GRAMOPHONE	ELECTRICAL GRAMOPHONES BEGIN TO REPLACE WIND-UP ONES	LONG-PLAYER VINYL DISCS INTRODUCED	'SINGLES' INTRODUCED	CDs BECOME POPULAR AND GRADUALLY REPLACE VINYL DISCS

Motion pictures, 1882

In Java, Indonesia, wayang shadow puppets have enthralled audiences for thousands of years and in Europe, magic lantern slides were popular from the 17th century onwards. However, it was during the 19th century that inventors began to experiment with ways of capturing both still and moving images.

The invention of film

In 1882, French scientist Étienne-Jules Marey devised a camera called the chronophotographe, which moved a single band of film past an aperture (an adjustable opening) at a regular speed. His film-strip was made of oiled paper, which ripped all too easily. At the end of the decade, photography **pioneer** George Eastman and colleague Hannibal Goodwin had the idea of making film-strips from **celluloid**, which was much tougher.

The Edison Kinetoscope. Customers could watch scenes, such as a man sneezing, through the viewer at the top.

Peepholes

Inventor Thomas Edison was also at work creating moving pictures. One of his employees, William K L Dickson, devised a mechanism which ran a 50ft strip of film past a viewing aperture. In 1891, Edison was able to **patent** the first public-access moving-image machine, the Kinetoscope. It had a peephole at the top for people to view the film. Kinetoscope 'parlours' opened in New York, London and Paris in 1894.

Screen shows

In France, in 1895, Auguste and Louis Lumière invented a projector, a device which could throw moving images on to a screen. Their first film in 1895 depicted workers leaving a factory in Lyon.

To those who watched it was like a miraculous vision. Edison too, using his own machines, opened an exhibition of 'projected motion pictures' in New York in 1896. The films on offer were a boxing match, a dancer, and waves on the seashore.

Film makers soon realized they needed to be more adventurous. In 1899 French magician Georges Méliès made short fairytale and science-fiction films, which were very popular. In 1903 Edison oversaw the production of the first film to tell a complete story. Directed by Edwin S Porter, it was called *The Great Train Robbery* and lasted 11 minutes. Using techniques that would soon become commonplace, Porter built up suspense by switching between scenes of the robbers escaping, and a posse being formed to bring them to justice.

At first films were silent, and accompanied by a pianist who played along in the cinema. During the 1920s sound was added, and in the 1930s the first colour films arrived. Today, the motion picture industry continues to generate billions of dollars and entertain the world.

An advert for the Lumière Brothers Parisian movie theatre. The scene on the screen is from a **slap-stick** *comedy called* The Sprinkler Sprinkled.

1882	1889	1889	1895	1903	1927
ÉTIENNE-JULES MAREY INVENTS MOVING PICTURE CHRONOPHOTOGRAPHE	GEORGE EASTMAN AND HANNIBAL GOODWIN USE CELLULOID FILM TO CAPTURE MOVING IMAGES	WILLIAM K L DICKSON AND THOMAS EDISON INVENT FIRST EFFICIENT MOVIE CAMERA AND KINETOSCOPE PROJECTOR	LOUIS AND AUGUSTE LUMIÈRE INVENT EFFICIENT FILM PROJECTOR	THE FIRST REAL FILM – *THE GREAT TRAIN ROBBERY*	THE FIRST FILM WITH SOUND, *THE JAZZ SINGER*, RELEASED BY WARNER BROTHERS

Hand-held camera, 1888

From cavemen to kings, people have longed to make a record of their likeness and depict the events of their lives. **Papyrus**, **parchment** and canvas portraits give us some ideas of what historical figures such as Ramesses II and Henry VIII look like. But skilled artists have always been expensive, and having a portrait painted was something only the rich could consider.

In the early 1700s, a German chemist noticed that sunlight caused some salts to darken. The idea that images formed by light could be captured by a chemical process took hold. During the early 19th century the first crude photographic images were caught on chemically-treated glass plates.

By the 1850s, Frenchman Louis Jacques Daguerre and Englishman William Fox Talbot had both invented photographic methods. These enabled millions of Europeans to have their portrait taken, and daring explorers to record details of their visits to faraway lands. But they were expensive, difficult to use and too heavy to carry around.

An instant money-maker

Eastman's success was partially due to his decisions to sell his cameras through massive advertising campaigns.

In 1888 American inventor and businessman George Eastman introduced a product that would make photography available to everyone. He called his box camera the Kodak No 1. Inside, there was a long strip of film, which had been coated with light-sensitive chemicals. The camera was so light it could be lifted easily with one hand. When the 100 shot film was finished the whole package was returned to Kodak, and the film was developed and printed. For the first time in history, people could record the events and milestones of their lives, in a way that could hardly be easier or cheaper. In 1900 Eastman sealed his success by introducing the Box Brownie camera – it cost $1 and sold 100,000 in its first year.

The Kodak Camera

"You press the button, we do the rest."

OR YOU CAN DO IT YOURSELF.

The only camera that anybody can use without instructions. As convenient to carry as an ordinary field glass   World-wide success.

The Kodak is for sale by all Photo stock dealers.

Send for the Primer, free.

The Eastman Dry Plate & Film Co.

Price, $25.00 — Loaded for 100 Pictures.   ROCHESTER, N. Y.

George Eastman (1854–1932)

As a child, American George Eastman invented toys and sold them to his friends. It was a fitting start to the life of a man who was to become a multi-millionaire. At the age of 23 he bought his first camera. He was quick to see that the complex, hefty mechanism could be updated with something more manageable.

Eastman never married. He was devoted to his mother, and treated his workforce well. In an age when workers were often treated harshly, he cut hours, provided night classes and healthcare, and even introduced a profit sharing scheme. He also gave over $100 million to charities and universities.

Into the future

The huge success of these cameras created a massive market for photography. During the 20th century further inventions such as cheap colour film and instant Polaroid snaps continued to make photography an internationally popular pastime.

Unlike most employers of the time, Eastman was kind and generous to his workforce.

In these days of auto-focus and self-winding film, photography has never been easier. Now, digital cameras are becoming common. The subject is captured on light sensitive **pixels**, which store the image as **binary data**. Downloaded onto a computer, the picture can be printed out on the spot or can be sent anywhere via email.

1827	1839	1888	1920s	1935	1947
JOSEPH NIÉPCE PRODUCES FIRST PHOTOGRAPH	LOUIS JACQUES DAGUERRE INVENTS DAGUERREOTYPE (SINGLE POSITIVE IMAGE) WILLIAM FOX TALBOT INVENTS CALOTYPE PROCESS (REPRODUCIBLE NEGATIVE IMAGE)	GEORGE EASTMAN PRODUCES FIRST MASS-MARKET, FILM-LOADED CAMERA	35MM FILM USED IN CAMERAS	KODACHROME COLOUR FILM INTRODUCED	POLAROID FILM MARKETED

Jukebox, 1889

The first jukebox was installed in the Palais Royal Saloon, San Francisco, in November 1889. Drinkers popped in a nickel to hear it play a **wax cylinder** recording of a song. This jukebox only had one piece of music, but it was such a success it took $1000 in its first six months.

Slot machines have been with us since the Ancient Greeks, who had coin-operated sacred water dispensers installed in temples. Machines which play music for a small fee also predate the jukebox. Many Victorian drinking houses had polyphons. They sounded like musical boxes, and played a chiming melody for a penny. Similar American machines, called nickelodeons, played a tune for a nickel. Automatic pianos and pipe organs were also fitted out to take the small change of music-minded drinkers.

Pre-recorded music

What was different about the Palais Royal Saloon's machine though, was that it played a pre-recorded piece of music. In 1905 a jukebox called the *Multiphone* offered its customers 24 different tunes, all on wax cylinders. The Multiphone was an impressive looking machine. The cylinders were held on a large wheel behind a glass case. When a choice was made the wheel revolved to play the cylinder selected, and music wafted out of the wooden cabinet.

The shellac disc

Wax cylinder jukeboxes were popular, but the jukebox really took off after 1927, when the American Automatic Music Instrument Company brought out a machine which played shellac discs called '78s' via an electric **amplifier** and speakers. (Shellac and vinyl discs were called 78s, 45s, or 33s, after the speed they revolved around the turntable. A 33, for example, revolved 33 times a minute.)

The 1940s and 1950s were a golden age for the jukebox. In America, in the late 1940s, jukeboxes were playing an extraordinary five billion records a year. Such companies as Wurlitzer and Rock-Ola made gaudy chrome-edged machines in tens of thousands. Lit by fluorescent and neon tubes, their curves reflected the sleek automobile styling of the time.

What's in a word?
Jukebox comes from a Creole/West African word *jook*, which either means dancing or wicked, depending on which dictionary you read!

A jukebox in an American diner in the 1940s. In the era before teenagers could afford gramophones and records, jukeboxes were an affordable way to hear favourite records.

As music recording technology evolved, 78s were replaced by 45s and then CDs. Today, most jukeboxes sit discreetly on the wall of cafés, pubs and bars – small rectangular boxes of plastic and glass. They may still be popular, but it is difficult to imagine today's functional electronic machines holding anything like the attraction of the garish, booming jukeboxes of the 40s and 50s.

1889	1905	1927	1989
FIRST JUKEBOX INSTALLED AT PALAIS ROYAL SALOON, SAN FRANCISCO	MULTI-CHOICE JUKEBOX, CALLED THE MULTIPHONE, INVENTED	AUTOMATIC MUSIC INSTRUMENT COMPANY INVENTS ELECTRIC AMPLIFIED JUKEBOX	WURLITZER PRODUCE FIRST CD JUKEBOX

Tape recorder, 1898

A tape recorder stores sound on a tape. The original idea came from a Danish electrical engineer Valdemar Poulsen. He intended it to be a telephone answering machine, but it went on to become an indispensable part of the home stereo unit.

How it works

Poulsen's tape recorder, invented in 1898, used a steel wire to record electrical impulses, and modern tape recorders still use this basic idea. They have a coil of wire encased in an iron sheath called a 'recording head'. When an electrical signal from a microphone or another form of recorded music such as a CD is sent to the recording head it produces a magnetic field, which changes according to the sound being sent to it. A plastic tape coated with a thin layer of metal particles passes over the recording head. The particles in the tape are affected by the changes in the magnetic field and form patterns which vary according to the sound.

When the tape is played back, a replay head (similar to the recording head) picks up these patterns and turns them into an electrical signal identical to the one that originally made the patterns. This signal is then fed to an **amplifier** and reproduced by a loudspeaker.

A reel-to-reel tape recorder from 1953. Anyone wanting to use the machine had to thread a tape from a spool around an array of tape heads, and guide wheels onto another spool.

The reel-to-reel

The first modern tape recorder was the magnetophone, developed by a German firm, AEG, in 1931. This was a type of recorder known as a reel-to-reel, because it carried one reel of magnetic plastic tape past its recording and playback heads on to another reel.

This technology was considerably improved in the late 1940s by the American companies 3M, which produced high quality magnetic tape, and Ampex, which made high-quality professional tape recorders.

In the 1940s sound recordings were made 'live' and directly to a master disc, which was then used to make copies of records to be sold to the public. Mistakes were very expensive, and no piece of music could last longer than the maximum length of the disc – four minutes. But in 1948, the popular American singer Bing Crosby began to record with 3M and Ampex equipment and within a year almost all professional recordings were made by tape. The advantages were obvious – tapes could record for a much longer time, and several performances could be captured on tape with the best 'spliced' (cut) together to make one complete song.

Reel-to-reels produced good recordings but were too bulky and fiddly to catch on to the same extent as gramophones. It was only in 1964, when Dutch electronics company Philips produced the 'compact cassette' that tape recorders began to appear in people's homes in vast numbers.

A better quality recording

The arrival of the Dolby noise reduction system in 1969, which cut down on the background hiss tapes produced, was another huge boost, as was the invention of the Sony Walkman and its many imitators. Both ensured tapes would be popular with music buyers for the rest of the century. Today, new mediums such as Digital Audio Tape and Digital Compact Cassette are replacing the humble compact cassette, but its cheapness and simplicity will see tapes and tape recorders around for a few more years yet.

1898	1931	1948	1964	1969	1979
VALDEMAR POULSEN INVENTED THE FIRST RECORDING DEVICE TO STORE SOUND ON TAPE	MAGNETOPHONE IS INVENTED. IT USED MAGNETIC PLASTIC TAPE TO STORE SOUND	BING CROSBY BEGINS TO RECORD ON MAGNETIC TAPE. THIS BECOMES STANDARD PRACTICE WITHIN A YEAR	PHILIPS INTRODUCES THE FIRST COMPACT CASSETTE	DOLBY NOISE REDUCTION GREATLY IMPROVES QUALITY OF TAPE RECORDINGS	SONY BEGINS TO SELL THE WALKMAN

Animation, 1900

Cartoons, or animations, work in the same way as motion pictures. But instead of real images captured **frame** by frame on film, illustrations are used, each one slightly different from the last.

Illusion of movement

The first cartoon animation in 1900 was part of a silent black and white film called *The Enchanted Drawing*, made by, and starring J Stuart Blackton, in America. In the film an artist draws a face, which seems to magically come to life, via cartoon animation.

In 1908, French director Emile Cohl produced *Fantasmagorie*, the first complete cartoon with its own story. New York producer John Bray made the first cartoon series, with the character Colonel Heeza Liar. But the cartoon that really caught the public's imagination was Winsor McCay's *Gertie the Dinosaur* of 1914. Barely five minutes long, it featured a cute prehistoric creature that audiences adored. McCay had hand-drawn each frame, which took him a whole year. This was clearly not the way forward.

Gertie the Dinosaur, created by American artist Winsor McCay in 1914, was immensely popular with cinema audiences.

At John Bray's studio, illustrator Earl Hurd came up with the idea of using 'cels' – pictures painted on to transparent **celluloid**. As with previous cartoons, each one was slightly different, and when run together produced the illusion of movement. But because the cels were transparent they could be placed on top of a single painted background. This made cartoons quicker and cheaper to make.

Walt Disney and Warner Brothers

Walt Disney, more than anyone else, was responsible for the success of the cartoon. Mickey Mouse first appeared in a cartoon named *Steamboat Willie* in 1928. Other characters, such as Donald Duck and Pluto the Dog, followed. But it was his films, more than anything else, that made Disney's reputation. *Snow White* (1937), *Dumbo* (1941) and *Bambi* (1942) are as popular with children now as they were when they first came out. Another film studio, Warner Brothers, made *Looney Tunes* and *Merrie Melodies* cartoons, with characters such as Daffy Duck and Bugs Bunny. The storylines were much more **slap-stick** and **surreal** than Disney's.

Walt Disney with his wife and Mickey Mouse at the Disney Studios in California, USA.

Modern animation

But, as television became popular in the 1950s and 1960s, cinema audiences dwindled. Film studios began making low-budget, low-quality cartoons for TV. Recently, cartoons have made a comeback. Matt Groening's *The Simpsons* is one of the most popular television programmes in the world. Each episode takes nearly a year to make. Disney, and other big studios still make feature-length cartoons.

Other cartoon techniques too, such as the computer animation used in the *Toy Story* films, and the plasticine models used in Aardman Animation's *Chicken Run*, continue to ensure that animation is still a major part of the film industry.

1900	1908	1914	1928	1995
THE ENCHANTED DRAWING – THE FIRST FILM TO FEATURE ANIMATION	*FANTASMAGORIE* – THE FIRST CARTOON ADVENTURE	CELS INVENTED BY EARL HURD	WALT DISNEY MAKES THE FIRST MICKEY MOUSE FILM	*TOY STORY*, THE FIRST FULLY COMPUTER-GENERATED FULL LENGTH FEATURE FILM, IS RELEASED

Electric microphone, 1924

Microphones convert sound waves from a voice or music into electric signals, which can then be carried down a telephone line, put through a loudspeaker, or recorded onto tape or disk.

Elvis Presley, Rock and Roll's first and biggest global star, in a late 1960s TV broadcast. Without a microphone, Presley would never have achieved the international popularity he did.

More than half the inventions in this book make use of microphones. Most of what you watch and listen to for entertainment, from film and television to any kind of recorded sound, and most live music, makes use of microphones. Even **space probes** carry them to catch the sounds of distant planets.

The microphone was invented by Alexander Graham Bell in 1876, as a vital part of the telephone. Called a carbon microphone, it picked up the sound of the human voice and reproduced it in a **receiver**. Carbon microphones worked in a similar way to today's microphones, but the sound they reproduced was tinny and distorted.

First recordings

The first recordings were made by mechanical sound recording devices, which did not use electricity. Instead of microphones they had large horns to capture a performance, and recorded this sound on a **wax cylinder** with a steel **stylus**. It was only in 1924 that the first recording and reproduction equipment was developed that made use of a microphone and electrical power.

This equipment was designed by two technicians named J P Maxfield and H C Harrison, of the American company AT&T. They used electrically powered microphones and sound recording equipment, which they called the 'orthophonic' system. This was a massive improvement on the previous method. The orthophonic system extended the range of recorded sound by a whole eight notes, and made recordings that were much clearer and more accurate. In 1925, the young record industry adopted electrical recording, and from then on, most records sold were made using a microphone.

Miking up

There has been a gradual improvement in the quality of microphones, and the business of 'miking' up particular instruments for studio and live performances has become a science in itself. Generally, studio recordings are made with microphones which are very sensitive and give maximum sound quality. These microphones are easily damaged, so live performances tend to make use of microphones which are more robust, but do not give such good quality reproduction.

How a microphone works

*This is a 'moving coil' microphone. Here is how it changes sound into an electrical signal, which is then boosted by an **amplifier** and turned back into sound by a loudspeaker.*

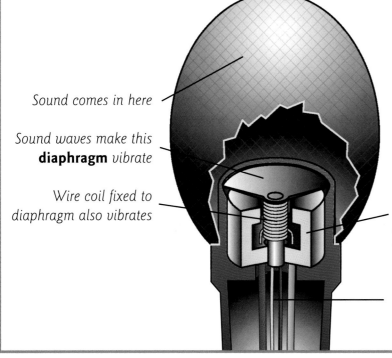

Sound comes in here

*Sound waves make this **diaphragm** vibrate*

Wire coil fixed to diaphragm also vibrates

Coil is surrounded by a magnet. As it moves it produces a varying electrical current

The current is carried by these wires to an amplifier

1876	1877	1924	1925
FIRST MICROPHONE INVENTED FOR USE IN TELEPHONES	SOUND FIRST CAPTURED ON DISC, USING HORN	J P MAXFIELD AND H C HARRISON DEVELOP ELECTRIC MICROPHONE	FIRST ELECTRIC MICROPHONE SOUND RECORDINGS SOLD IN SHOPS

Television, 1925

The telephone and **wireless** were invented in the last quarter of the 19th century, and if sound could be carried by wire, or sent through the air in invisible waves, then why not moving images? But firstly, a camera had to record a scene and translate it into electrical signals that could be **transmitted**. Secondly, a **receiver** had to transform these signals back into an image.

Breaking down images

The first breakthrough came in 1884 with German inventor Paul Nipkow. He realized that an image could not be transmitted whole, and had to be broken down into tiny pieces and then reassembled. To do this he invented a scanning disc. This device rotated at 600 times per minute, recording an image bit by bit, and transforming the areas of light and shade it picked up into electrical signals via a **photo-electrical cell**.

Twenty years later, Russian scientist Boris Rosing created the first crude TV system by using Nipkow's disc to record a still image, and a cathode ray tube to display this image on a screen. Invented in 1897 by Ferdinand Braun in Germany, the cathode ray tube used a beam of **electrons** to 'paint' a picture on a **fluorescent** screen.

Baird's television apparatus, 1926. Equipment such as this was used in the first public demonstration of moving television images.

John Logie Baird

After the First World War John Logie Baird, a Scotsman working in London, worked on his own television using a bizarre collection of objects such as hatboxes and coffin lids as equipment. He developed Nipkow's scanning disc to a stage where it could record and reproduce a moving image. Because of this he is generally regarded as the inventor of television. Although Baird's system was used to make the first broadcast programmes, it was abandoned in the 1930s because the image it produced was too blurred and the equipment too cumbersome.

By the 1950s, television screens had grown bigger in order to compete with cinema.

Quality TV

In 1923, American engineer Vladimir Zworykin invented a device called an iconoscope. It broke down an image into hundreds of thousands of elements, and played an essential part in the first practical TV camera. In 1924 Zworykin also developed a television receiver he called the kinescope, which used Ferdinand Braun's cathode ray tube. Zworykin's inventions were publicly demonstrated in Pittsburgh in 1929 and paved the way for the all-electric TV system.

National broadcasting began in the UK, USA and Germany in the 1930s, but TV only really caught on in the 1950s and 60s. Today there are few homes in the developed world without a television, and watching TV is the world's number one leisure activity.

1884	1897	1923	1924	1925	1929
PAUL NIPKOW INVENTS AN IMAGE SCANNING MACHINE	FERDINAND BRAUN INVENTS THE CATHODE RAY TUBE, AN ESSENTIAL PART OF THE TV SET	VLADIMIR ZWORYKIN INVENTS THE ICONOSCOPE, THE BASIS FOR THE MODERN TV CAMERA	VLADIMIR ZWORYKIN INVENTS THE KINESCOPE, THE BASIS FOR THE MODERN TV SET	JOHN LOGIE BAIRD GIVES FIRST PUBLIC DEMONSTRATION OF A MOVING IMAGE ON A TELEVISION SCREEN	VLADIMIR ZWORYKIN GIVES THE FIRST DEMONSTRATION OF HIS TV SYSTEM IN PITTSBURGH

Electric guitar, 1931

The electric guitar owes its success to two essential attributes. Firstly, it is an easy instrument to learn how to play. Many pop songs have only three or four basic chords, which can be easily learned on the guitar. Secondly, it is an immensely versatile instrument. In the hands of a competent player, it can produce a vast range of sounds.

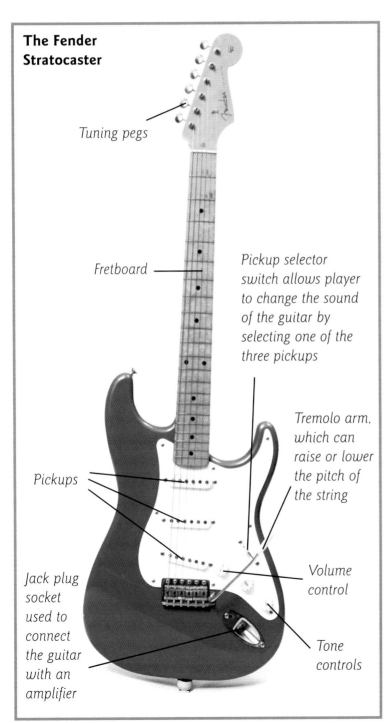

The Fender Stratocaster

Tuning pegs

Fretboard

Pickup selector switch allows player to change the sound of the guitar by selecting one of the three pickups

Pickups

Tremolo arm, which can raise or lower the pitch of the string

Jack plug socket used to connect the guitar with an amplifier

Volume control

Tone controls

The first guitars were invented in Spain in the 15th century. Made of wood with gut (animal intestine) strings, they were light enough to be carried anywhere, and could be played as a solo instrument, or used to accompany a singer.

Electrical advances

Microphones and loudspeakers in the early 20th century revolutionized musical performances, and dance bands especially made immediate use of these. It enabled singers to make themselves heard over both larger bands and bigger audiences.

Acoustic guitars are quiet instruments, so guitarists in a band would struggle to be heard. At first, band-leaders employed two or three guitarists to make the instrument cut through, but the problem was eventually solved by using a 'pickup' with a guitar.

The pickup line

A pickup is a tightly bound bundle of wire, wrapped around a magnet. A vibrating string changes the magnetic field in the pickup, and this produces an electric signal. When this signal is fed through an **amplifier** and loudspeaker, a note can be heard. American musical instrument maker Lloyd Loar is credited with inventing the pickup in the 1920s.

The first models

The first purpose-built electric guitar was produced by George Beauchamp, Paul Barth and Adolph Rickenbacker in 1931. Their instruments were called 'frying pans' because they resembled this cooking implement.

The electric guitar really took off though, in the late 1940s. American manufacturer Leo Fender produced a solid-body instrument he called the Broadcaster in 1948. This later became much better known as the Telecaster. In 1952 the rival Gibson guitar company produced a much more refined instrument called the Les Paul, named after the guitarist who helped to develop it. Fender produced another guitar called the Stratocaster in 1954. These three instruments remain the most played electric guitars to this day.

Rock musician Noel Gallagher, of Oasis, playing a Gibson Les Paul. Originally produced in 1952, this instrument is still one of the most popular makes of electric guitar.

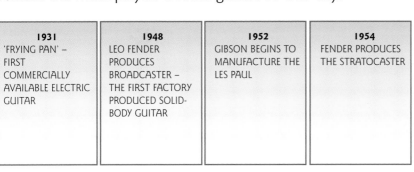

1931	1948	1952	1954
'FRYING PAN' – FIRST COMMERCIALLY AVAILABLE ELECTRIC GUITAR	LEO FENDER PRODUCES BROADCASTER – THE FIRST FACTORY PRODUCED SOLID-BODY GUITAR	GIBSON BEGINS TO MANUFACTURE THE LES PAUL	FENDER PRODUCES THE STRATOCASTER

Transistor radio, 1953

Radio messages were first broadcast for entertainment in the 1900s. During the 1920s most European and American households had radio sets, and radio broadcasts were a regular part of family life – much like watching television is today.

Sound waves

As with many other electrical items of the time, radios made use of components called valves, designed by Lee DeForest in 1907. These valves were large glass tubes containing glowing wires that acted as signal **amplifiers**. Radio valves translated the radio wave signals the radio aerial picked up into something that could be heard on a loudspeaker. But the size and fragility of valves meant that any equipment that used them was usually large, heavy and easily broken.

A family listening to a cricket match on the radio in 1932. These huge sets were very popular, but not remotely portable.

In 1947, three physicists with the Bell Telephone company – John Bardeen, Walter Brattain and William Shockley – invented the transistor. Like the valve, the transistor could amplify electronic signals, and could also be used as an electronic switch. But it was much smaller, faster, lighter, more robust, and cheaper to make and use. Transistors revolutionized electronics, and paved the way for every modern electronic device from the computer to the mobile phone. They were also directly responsible for the transistor radio.

The first transistors were used to produce hearing aids. In 1953 P E Haggerty, president of Texas Instruments, decided that they could be put to use in radio sets. Together with a small Indianapolis electronics manufacturer called IDEA, and a firm of industrial designers called Painter, Teague and Petertil, they produced the pocket-sized Regency TR-1. First sold in November 1954, the TR-1 cost a hefty $49 – nearly £300 in today's money. Powered by a small battery, it enabled its owner to listen to radio broadcasts anywhere.

A source of information

In the early 1950s, when America and Russia were deeply hostile to each other, many people expected nuclear war to break out at any moment, and listened to radio news wherever they were. On a lighter note, children and teenagers also had more opportunity to listen to music their parents disliked – especially from the mid-50s onwards, when rock and roll became hugely popular.

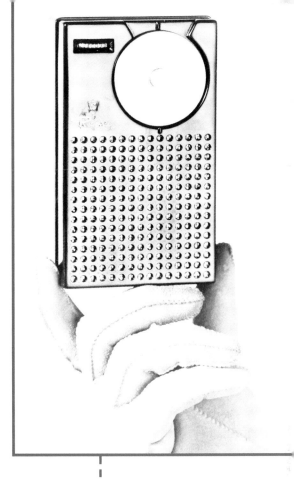

By the mid-1950s Japanese manufacturers such as Sony were also producing transistor radios, which were much cheaper than American models, and soon dominated the market. In later years, researchers at the huge IBM company were given TR-1 radios as inspiration, and told to put transistors into computers. This initial link enabled Texas Instruments to make many millions of dollars selling their transistors to IBM.

The Regency TR-1 transistor radio first hit the shops in 1954. The arrival of rock and roll aided the success of the transistor radio immensely.

Over the years transistor radios became smaller and cheaper, and completely eclipsed the valve radio. Today, valves are mainly used in specialist hi-fi equipment, and electric guitar amplifiers. Their warm tone is considered superior to transistor-based reproduction equipment.

1920s	1947	1952	1953	1954	1955
VALVE RADIO SETS BECOME HUGELY POPULAR	JOHN BARDEEN, WALTER BRATTAIN AND WILLIAM SHOCKLEY INVENTED THE TRANSISTOR	TRANSISTOR FIRST USED IN HEARING AIDS	REGENCY TR-1, WORLD'S FIRST TRANSISTOR RADIO INVENTED	TR-1 FIRST SOLD IN SHOPS	JAPANESE MANUFACTURERS SUCH AS SONY PRODUCE HIGHLY SUCCESSFUL TRANSISTOR RADIOS

Video recorder, 1956

When television first became popular in the 1950s, all programmes were 'live'. From the news to the adverts, soap operas to singing stars, performers and presenters had to stand in front of the cameras and get everything right first time. This made broadcasting a very stressful business.

It was possible to pre-record programmes. John Logie Baird, for example, had captured some of his broadcasts on **wax discs**, but the playback quality was very poor. The solution lay in technology that had been developed to capture sound – the tape recorder and its magnetic tape. The first usable sound-recording machines were made in the 1930s by German companies AEG and BASF. After the Second World War, this technology was taken up by American companies Ampex and 3M, who used it to develop both sound and video-recording equipment.

How a video works

Videos pick up signals from TV broadcasts, and store them on magnetic tape, in the same way that tape recorders store sound. When you record a programme a loop of tape is pulled out of your video cassette and wrapped around a spinning recording head. The head records the picture signal across the width of the tape, and sound is recorded along one edge.

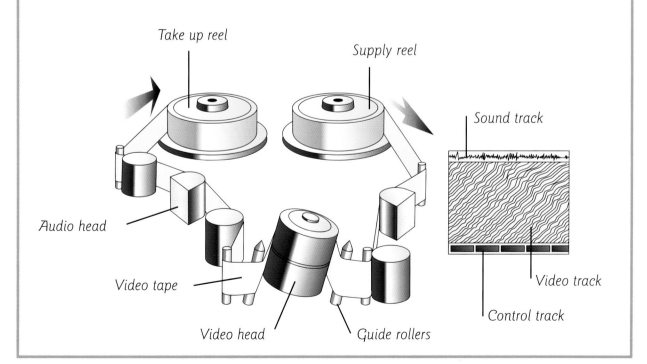

Take up reel

Supply reel

Sound track

Audio head

Video tape

Video head

Guide rollers

Video track

Control track

To register effectively, TV signals have to be recorded on a tape at very high speeds. The first machines ran tape over the **recording heads** at such a high speed that they got through huge reels of tape in minutes. But Ampex realized that they could produce the same effect by revolving the recording head at speed, rather than the tape itself.

Reel-to-reel

The company demonstrated the first practical videotape recording machine, the reel-to-reel Ampex Mark IV, in 1956. Developed by a team led by Alexander M Poniatoff and Charles P Ginsburg, it was first used in broadcasting in 1958. Programmes could be recorded at one time, and then broadcast at another.

The first video recorders were too expensive and large for home use – the Ampex Mark IV, for example, was about the size of a small car. But from the 1960s the race was on to produce a machine that would allow the TV viewer to record programmes when they were out.

An early home video machine from the 1970s. Initially, consumers had three formats to choose from, but eventually the VHS type machine shown here became the standard.

Modern systems

The first affordable and reasonable quality home recorders appeared in the shops during the early 1970s. In 1972 Philips produced their VCR system, in 1975 Sony introduced the Betamax, and in 1976 JVC turned out the VHS cassette. The VHS offered the longest playing time per tape, and by the start of the 1980s, it had become the most popular format, and became the standard video player.

1926	1956	1972	1975	1976
JOHN LOGIE BAIRD **PATENTS** WAX DISC VIDEO RECORDER	AMPEX PRODUCES ITS MARK IV VIDEO RECORDER, FOR USE BY TV BROADCASTERS	PHILIPS INTRODUCE THE VCR – THE FIRST AFFORDABLE HOME VIDEO RECORDER	SONY INTRODUCES BETAMAX FORMAT	JVC INTRODUCES VHS FORMAT

Computer games, 1958

The computer game world of magic forests, mad monkeys, exploding guts and spaceships is littered with dismal failures, setbacks and glittering triumphs – and not just on screen.

The first person to invent a video game didn't **patent** the idea. In 1958, Willy Higinbotham, a physicist at the Brookhaven National Laboratory in New York State, came up with a simple video-screen-based table tennis game. In devising the game, Higinbotham used computer technology that had been originally developed during the Second World War to work out the **trajectories** of missiles.

Steve Russell

Three years later Massachusetts Institute of Technology researcher Steve Russell began working with a huge computer called the PDP-1. Unlike any other computer at the time, this one had a TV screen monitor and typewriter keyboard. Russell was a science-fiction enthusiast, and made use of the PDP-1 to devise his own computer game.

He wrote a program called Spacewar, where two competing players controlled spaceships which fired lasers. At first they used the computer keyboard, but Russell and his colleagues soon devised a hand-held set of buttons, which controlled the action on the screen much more effectively. Russell's game was a huge success among his colleagues, and spread rapidly through the research facilities of the USA. But in the early 1960s the computers that could accommodate Spacewar were so big and expensive, it was impossible to imagine the game going any further.

How Atari began

Technology was moving on, and computers became smaller and cheaper. American engineer Nolan Bushnell had come across Spacewar at the University of Utah, and he devised his own version of the game for amusement arcades. Called 'Computer Space', Bushnell sold it to an arcade game manufacturer. But the game was considered too difficult, and was not popular.

Frustrated with his lack of success, Bushnell set up his own company Atari, named after a term used in the Japanese board game named Go. Together with computer programmer Al Alcorn, Bushnell devised a tennis game called Pong. Arcade game manufacturers showed no interest, so Bushnell began to build and sell these machines himself. The game was an immediate success and when a home **console** version of Pong was produced in 1974 it became the fastest-selling game in America. Other games such as Frogger and Centipede followed. In the late 1970s, Space Invaders, where ranks of skull-like alien faces descended on ray guns at the bottom of the screen, became a craze that swept the world.

A computer game from the 1970s. Despite their lack of sophistication, these slow, two dimensional games were still immensely popular.

The Japanese market

In the early 1980s a Japanese designer working for the Nintendo company set about changing the face of video games. His name was Shigeru Miyamoto and he had grown up reading Japanese *Manga* comics. Here, specific, recognizable characters overcame myriad adversities in a well-defined, imaginary world. Miyamoto applied this concept to video games, producing the hugely popular Super Mario Brothers, and Donkey Kong. From Sonic's Hedgehog to Lara Croft, other computer games followed suit. Today, the industry is dominated by Japanese companies such as Sony, Nintendo and Sega.

1958	1961	1971	1974	1985	1994
WILLY HIGINBOTHAM DEVISES VIDEO TABLE TENNIS – THE FIRST VIDEO GAME	STEVE RUSSELL AND COLLEAGUES CREATE SPACEWAR	NOLAN BUSHNELL CREATES COMPUTER SPACE – THE FIRST ARCADE VIDEO GAME	ATARI'S PONG HOME VIDEO GAME BECOMES THE FASTEST SELLING TOY IN AMERICA	NINTENDO DEVISES CHARACTER-BASED GAMES SUCH AS SUPER MARIO	SONY PRODUCES THE PLAYSTATION WHICH BECOMES THE BEST SELLING HOME VIDEO FORMAT FOR THE REST OF THE DECADE

Compact disc, 1965

In the early 1980s physicist James Russell, and the technicians of the Sony and Philips companies provided the world with the compact disc (CD). Russell, who lived in America, actually invented the compact disc in 1965. He was a keen music enthusiast, and was convinced there were better ways of storing music than the **vinyl LP**, which was noisy, and wore out with repeated plays.

Storing information

Russell was familiar with computer technology, and understood the way computers store information in a series of 0s and 1s. (This is called **binary** or **digital data**.) Music can also be **sampled** by a computer and recorded in this format.

Russell worked out a way of storing sound as binary data, representing the 0s and 1s as a series of microscopic grooves and flat areas on a spinning disc. These grooves and flat areas are 'read' by a tiny laserbeam, which is reflected by the flat areas and not by the pits. This produces a flickering signal that can be changed into an electrical signal, **amplified** and then reproduced by a loudspeaker. Because there is no physical contact between CD and CD player, the information on a CD can never wear out.

When CDs were launched in the early 1980s, many people bought recordings they already had as vinyl LPs all over again. Groups such as Pink Floyd, who had already had immense record sales for their Dark Side of the Moon LP, made millions of dollars in additional CD sales.

Dutch company Philips further developed the idea, and initially used it to store video programmes. By the late 1970s, Philips was working together with the Sony corporation of Japan to produce a **commercially** available disc that played music.

CD replaces the LP

The new CD was first demonstrated in 1979, and the new music format hit the shops in 1982. It was a success right from the start and throughout the decade sales of vinyl tailed off as record buyers switched to CDs.

The CD's audio sensitivity is 30 times greater than that of the vinyl LP. It is much smaller, and therefore more convenient to store. It can carry much more music on a single disc. Yet some people find the sound the CD produces is not as pleasing to the ear as the vinyl LP. CDs may reproduce clear, distortion-free music, but many people feel they lack the warmth and depth of old-fashioned vinyl.

How a CD works

A CD player uses a laserbeam to 'read' a series of grooves and flat areas on a CD as areas of light and dark. It converts this information into an electrical signal which can then be amplified and reproduced through a loudspeaker as sound.

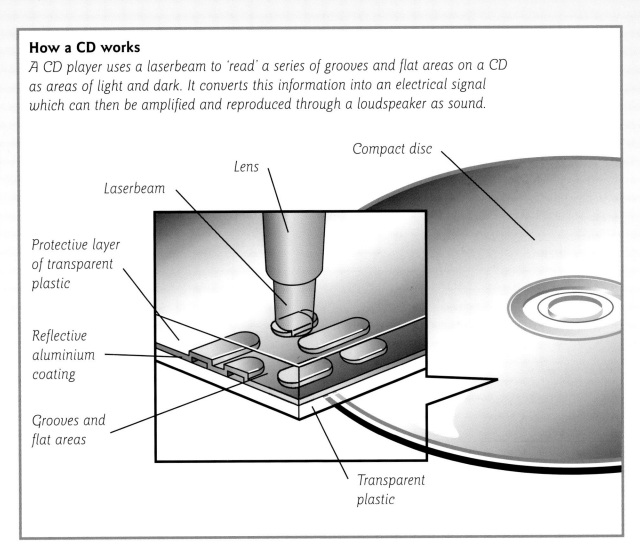

Compact disc

Lens

Laserbeam

Protective layer of transparent plastic

Reflective aluminium coating

Grooves and flat areas

Transparent plastic

1965	1979	1982	1983
JAMES RUSSELL INVENTS CD FORMAT	PHILIPS AND SONY DEMONSTRATE THE AUDIO CD, WHICH THEY HAD DEVELOPED TOGETHER	CDs AND CD PLAYERS GO ON SALE IN JAPAN	CDs AND CD PLAYERS GO ON SALE IN EUROPE AND AMERICA

Digital camcorder, 1995

During the 1980s and 1990s videotape cameras, or camcorders, began to rival photography as a popular way of recording the events in people's lives. Camcorders convert images into electrical signals which are then stored on a tape as a pattern of magnetic particles. This is known as **analogue** recording. Widespread ownership of home video recorders since the 1980s meant these videos could be viewed almost as easily as still photographs.

Sony's digital video camera is no bigger than a personal stereo. Despite its size, this miniature camera still has an LCD screen, and even a speaker, for instant playback of both sound and image.

The first camcorders came on to the home market in the 1970s. At the time they were considered to be marvels of **microtechnology**, although today they look big and clumsy. They recorded images on standard-sized VHS cassettes – the same ones that most people use in their video recorders today.

As camcorder technology improved, tapes became smaller. First came the VHS-C, a chunky, palm-sized cassette, which enabled the cameras to downsize accordingly. Then, even thinner, music-cassette sized tapes, known as 8mm were introduced, which allowed camcorders to be smaller still.

The mega-pixel sensor

The invention of digital camcorders began in 1986, when Kodak developed the mega-**pixel** sensor – a way of recording images as **digital** information. It could record 1.4 million different elements of light and shade, which was enough to produce a print that was comparable in quality to a photograph.

Sony developed the first home digital video cameras in 1995. They used similar-sized 8mm tape to the analogue camcorders, but the quality of the recorded image was much sharper. They were also lighter and smaller, and the images they recorded could be downloaded on to home computer to be edited and copied over and over again, with no noticeable loss of quality.

The way forward

As technology improves it will soon be possible to record an event, and send it, via email, or even simultaneously via a mobile phone modem to another computer or digital video recorder. The first digital camcorders cost anything between £4000–10,000 but now they can be bought for under £1000 and they show every sign of replacing the much cheaper analogue camcorders.

In 2000 Sony introduced the MD Discam, the first home-use camcorder to use a disc to record. As with a music CD, using a disc-based camcorder means that you can immediately find which part of the video you want. You can also edit your video on the spot, erasing any scenes you don't like, at the press of a button. But currently there is one major disadvantage. Analogue and digital camcorders using tape can capture hours of moving images, whereas the disc in the MD Discam can only store up to 20 minutes of information.

1970s	1986	1995	1999	2000
FIRST ANALOGUE CAMCORDERS	KODAK DEVELOPS MEGA-PIXEL SENSOR TO CAPTURE HIGH QUALITY DIGITAL IMAGES	SONY INTRODUCES DCR-VX1000 – THE FIRST COMMERCIALLY AVAILABLE DIGITAL CAMCORDER	'BACKWARDS COMPATIBLE' DIGITAL8 CAMCORDERS INTRODUCED, WHICH PLAY BOTH ANALOGUE AND DIGITAL TAPES	SONY INTRODUCES MD DISCAM DIGITAL CAMCORDER, WHICH USES MINIDISC INSTEAD OF TAPE

Timeline

c. 1000	Chinese discover gunpowder and make fireworks
1709	Bartolomeo Cristofori invents piano
1827	Joseph Niépce produces first photograph
1876	First microphone invented for use in telephone
1877	Thomas Edison invents phonograph
1882	Étienne-Jules Marey invents moving picture chronophotographe
1884	Paul Nipkow invents an image scanning machine
1887	Emile Berliner invents gramophone
1888	George Eastman produces first mass-market, film-loaded camera
1889	George Eastman and Hannibal Goodwin use **celluloid** film to capture moving images
	First jukebox installed at Palais Royal Saloon, San Francisco
1890s	American newspapers begin to produce comic colour **supplements**
1897	Ferdinand Braun invents the cathode ray tube, an essential part of the TV set
1898	Valdemar Poulsen invented the first recording device to store sound on tape
1900	*The Enchanted Drawing* – the first film to feature animation
1903	The first real film – *The Great Train Robbery*
1920s	Valve radio sets become hugely popular
1925	John Logie Baird gives first public demonstration of a moving image on a television screen
	First electric microphone sound recordings sold in shops
1926	John Logie Baird **patents wax disc** video recorder

1927	The first film with sound, *The Jazz Singer*, released by Warner Brothers
1928	Walt Disney makes the first Mickey Mouse film
1931	'Frying pan' – first commercially available electric guitar
1935	Kodachrome colour film introduced
1938	Superman appears in *Action Comics*, and is a huge success
1948	Long-player vinyl discs introduced
1953	Regency TR-1, world's first transistor radio invented
1958	Computer developed that can play chess
	Willy Higinbotham devises video table tennis – the first video game
1964	Philips introduces the first compact cassette
1965	James Russell invents CD format
1972	Philips introduce the VCR – the first affordable home video recorder
1979	Sony begins to sell the Walkman
1982	CDs and CD players go on sale in Japan
1986	Kodak develops mega-**pixel** sensor to capture high quality digital images
1994	Sony produces the PlayStation which becomes the best selling home video format for the rest of the decade
1995	Sony introduces DCR-VX1000 – the first commercially available digital camcorder
2000	Sony introduces MD Discam digital camcorder, which uses minidisc instead of tape

Glossary

acoustic guitar a guitar which uses a large sound box to make it audible, rather than a pickup and amplifier

amplifier a device used to increase volume in hi-fi systems or musical instruments

amplify to make louder

analogue recording a form of recording in which sound or pictures are represented by a particular strength of electric current

binary data information made up of two numbers, i.e. 0 and 1

block-printing a form of printing which uses engraved blocks coated with ink

caricature an exaggerated imitation of something, intended to be amusing

celluloid a type of transparent plastic used in film

commercial something which is sold by a company to make a profit

console an instrument panel

diaphragm a thin disc that vibrates in response to sound waves

digital recording a form of recording in which sound or pictures are represented by binary numbers

electrons tiny particles which are part of an atom, and which are an essential element of electricity

fluorescent screen a screen which glows when it is hit by electrons

frame a single image in a role of film

intestines long, tube-like part of the gut in animals

ivory a hard, white substance made from elephant or walrus tusks

literate the ability to read and write

lute string instrument, where the strings are plucked by hand like a guitar

microtechnology the science of producing machines that are immensely small

papyrus a form of paper made from papyrus plant

parchment the skin of a goat or sheep which can be written or painted on

patent an official document confirming ownership of a particular invention

photo-electrical cell an electrical device which is sensitive to light

pioneer someone who is first, or among the first, to do a particular activity

pixel a tiny cell which makes up the smallest part of a picture on a television screen

pneumatic something which uses high-pressure air to make it work

public address system a combination of microphones, amplifiers and loudspeakers used by public speakers or musicians to amplify sound and speech for a large crowd

receiver a type of electronic device which can pick up electrical signals, such as those transmitting sound and pictures

recording head part of a tape recorder or video where electric signals are transferred to tape

reed instrument a musical instrument which uses a thin piece of cane to make a sound

sample to take a small part of something

satire a type of entertainment in which topical subjects are made fun of

slap-stick a form of comedy which relies on physical action

space probe an unmanned spacecraft sent beyond Earth's orbit to explore other worlds

stylus a pointed metal device which translates the grooves in a record into an electrical signal which can be turned into sound

supplement an additional part of a newspaper

surreal something which is strange and dream-like

tabloid a paper size of around 30cm (12 inches) x 40cm (16 inches)

trajectory the path that a flying object takes

transmit to send out a signal via radio waves or wires

vinyl LP a device which stores recorded sound in the form of grooves etched into a plastic (vinyl) disc

viol an instrument similar to a violin

wax cylinder a device which records sound by etching vibrations onto wax

wax disc a device used to record images or sound before the invention of magnetic tape

wireless a device which picks up radio waves and turns them into sound (another word for radio)

Index

Titles in the *GREAT INVENTIONS* series include:

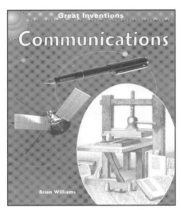

Hardback   0 431 13240 2

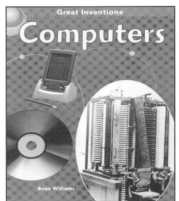

Hardback   0 431 13241 0

Hardback   0 431 13233 X

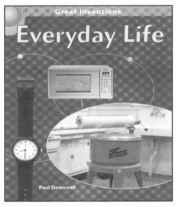

Hardback   0 431 13232 1

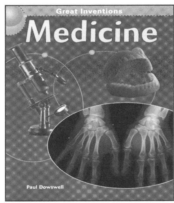

Hardback   0 431 13230 5

Hardback   0 431 13242 9

Hardback   0 431 13243 7

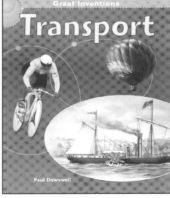

Hardback   0 431 13231 3

Find out about the other titles in this series on our website www.heinemann.co.uk/library